Penguin Books
Small Dreams of a Scorpion

Spike Milligan was born at Ahmednagar in India in 1919. He
received his first education in a tent in the Hyderabad Sindh
desert and graduated from there through a series of Roman
Catholic schools in India and England to the Lewisham
Polytechnic. Always something of a playboy, he then plunged
into the world of Show Business, seduced by his first stage
appearance, at the age of eight, in the nativity play of his Poona
convent school. He began his career as a band musician but has
since become famous as a humorous script writer and actor both
in films and broadcasting. He was one of the main figures in and
behind the infamous Goon Show. Among the films he has
appeared in are: *Suspect, Invasion, Postman's Knock* and
Milligan at Large. Spike Milligan has also published *The Little
Potboiler, Silly Verse for Kids* (a Puffin book), *Dustbin of Milligan,
A Book of Bits, The Bed-Sitting Room* (a play), *The Bald Twit
Lion, A Book of Milliganimals* (also in Puffins), *Puckoon* and
Adolf Hitler: My Part in His Downfall (both Penguin books).
He is married, has three children and lives in London.

small dreams of a scorpion

a scorpion

poems by spike milligan

with illustrations by
Spike and Laura Milligan

PENGUIN BOOKS

Penguin Books Ltd, Harmondsworth,
Middlesex, England
Penguin Books Inc., 7110 Ambassador Road,
Baltimore, Maryland 21207, U.S.A.
Penguin Books Australia Ltd, Ringwood,
Victoria, Australia

First published by M. & J. Hobbs in association with Michael Joseph 1972
Published in Penguin Books 1973
Copyright © Spike Milligan Productions Ltd, 1972

Made and printed in Great Britain by Hazell Watson & Viney Ltd, Aylesbury, Bucks
Set in Monophoto Ehrhardt

This book is dedicated to my mother
who spent a lifetime dedicated to me

Contents

Introduction	13
The Soldiers at Lauro	17
Death Wish	18
On observing a lone eagle	20
Manic Depression	22
Indian Boyhood	24
Myxomatosis	26
Me	28
The Children of Aberfan	30
Values '67	32
To Robert Graves	34
Opus I	36
Oberon	38
The New Rose	40
Values '68	42
Titikaka	43
Opus II	44
Love Song	46
Truth	48
Korea	50
I once – as a child	52
Onos	53
D.D.T.	54
2B or not 2B	56
The Dog Lovers	58
True Love	60
Christmas 1970	62
Opus III	65
England, Home and Beauty for Sale	66
Goliath	67
New Members Welcome	68
Hope	70
Metropolis	72
The Future	74
Unto us	76
Ulster, Derry 1972	78
The Incurable	80
Mirror, Mirror	81

Plastic Woman   82
Spring Song   84
If I die in War   86
God made night   87

Acknowledgements

The following poems originally appeared in
The Bedside Milligan: Titikaka, Values '67, Korea,
'Manic Depression', 'Christmas 1970', 'On
observing a lone eagle'.
The poem 'Myxomatosis' previously appeared in
Milligan's Ark.
The poem 'England, Home and Beauty for Sale'
was first published in *Sennet*.
The illustrations on pages 25, 33, 64, 69 and 77
are by Laura Milligan.

Introduction

There comes a time in every man's life when he stops laughing and starts to grind under the yoke of contemporary pressures. In this case, a wife, four children, a dog called Fred Flora McDonald, a cat called Kangaroo, Mr Heath, Mr Wilson, the Liberal Party, the Department of Inland Revenue, the breathalyser, etc. – (etc. being the worst) – they have all brought me to an impasse where I decided the only way to save my soul was to cleanse it with some serious verse which would take the police off my back and stop them searching me for funny poems.

The result of this change in personality is found within the confines of this book. Some of the poems were written by dropping 800 English words into a sack, taking them out one at a time and calling them by their names like 'Hello Sailor', or 'It only happens all the time', but seriously though folks, I find that I can say more pertinent things in writing serious verse and consequently have indulged myself in them a little.

My publishers being partially out of their minds have subscribed to printing this book and issuing a limited number of copies on various bookstalls throughout the British Empire, which these days goes as far as Islington.

I hope you enjoy them, but if you don't by the time you have found out it will be too late and the money will be in my Post Office Book.

NOTE: Please ignore the spelling and punctuation, – I did!

P.S. All rights, assignations, fire squads etc., should queue up outside Michael Joseph, Bedford Square and wait for the first one to come out.

Spike Milligan

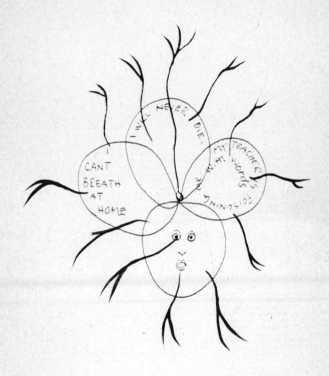

The Soldiers at Lauro

Young are the dead
Like babies they lie
The wombs they blest once
Not healed dry
And yet – too soon
Into each space
A cold earth falls
On colder face.
Quite still they lie
These fresh reeds
Clutched in earth
Like winter seeds
But these will not bloom
When called by spring
To burst with leaf
And blossoming
They will sleep on
In silent dust
As crosses rot
And memories rust.

Italy 1943

Death Wish

Bury me anywhere,
Somewhere near a tree
Some place where a horse will graze
And gallop over me.
Bury me
Somewhere near a stream,
When she floods her banks
I'll give her thanks
For reaching out to me.
So bury me – bury me
In my childhood scene;
But please –
don't burn me
In Golders Green.

Italy 1944

On observing a lone eagle
in the sky from
a trench in Tunisia

A bird a'flight
   Her wings spread wide
The soul of a man
   With his bonds untied
Beyond the plough
   The spade, the hod,
The bird flies,
   In the face of God.
Yet we with reason
   Bright as day
Forever tread
   An earthbound clay.

Tunisia 1943

GOD WHY DID YOU DRAW
ME SO BADLY

Manic Depression

The pain is too much
A thousand grim winters
   grow in my head.
In my ears
   the sound of the
   coming dead.
All seasons
All sane
All living
All pain.
No opiate to lock still
   my senses
Only left,
   the body locked tenses.

                St Luke's Hospital
                Psychiatric Wing, 1953/4

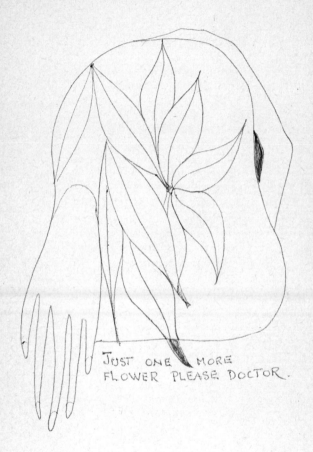

JUST ONE MORE
FLOWER PLEASE DOCTOR.

Indian Boyhood

What happened to the boy I was?
Why did he run away?
And leave me old and thinking, like
There'd been no yesterday?
What happened then?
Was I that boy
Who laughed and swam in the bund*?
Is there no going back?
No recompense?
Is there nothing?
No refund?

19 May 1959

*A canal in Poona

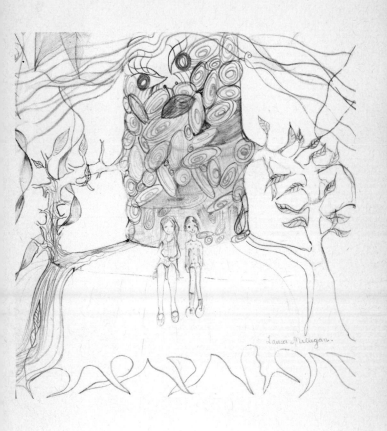

Myxomatosis

A baby rabbit
With eyes full of pus
Is the work of scientific us.

Myxamatosis

A baby rabbit
With eyes full of pus
Is the work of scientific
                    us.

Me

Born screaming small into this world –
Living I am
Occupational therapy twixt birth and death –
What was I before?
What will I be next?
What am I now?
Cruel answer carried in the jesting mind
        of a careless God.
I will not bend and grovel
When I die. If He says my sins are myriad
I will ask why He made me so imperfect
And he will say 'My chisels were blunt'.
I will say '*Then why did you make so
        many of me*'.

Bethlehem Hospital
Highgate 1966

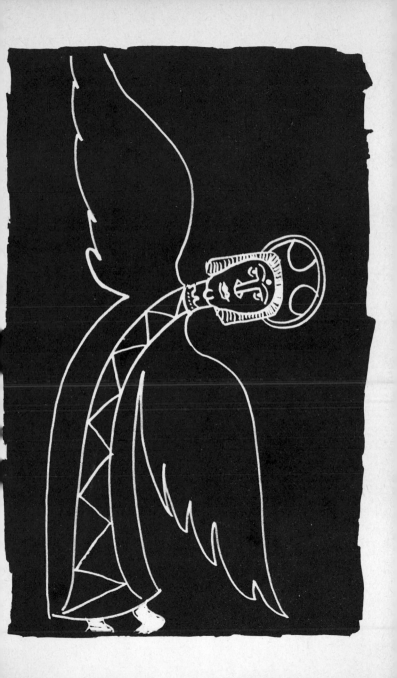

The Children of Aberfan

And now they will go
    wandering
Away from coal black earth,
The clean white children,
    holy as the Easter rose,
Away from the empty sludge-filled
    desks,
Away from the imprisoned spring
    that opened its mouth
    to breathe air
    and moved a black mountain
    to find it.
So,
Away they shall go – the children,
    wandering – wondering
    more loved
    more wanted
    than ever.
I don't burn coal any more.

October 1966

Values '67

Pass by citizen
    don't look left or right
Keep those drip dry eyes straight ahead.
A tree? Chop it down – it's a danger
    to lightning!
Pansies calling for water,
    Let 'em die – queer bastards –
Seek comfort in the scarlet, labour
    saving plastic rose
    Fresh with the fragrance of Daz!
Sunday! Pray citizen;
    Pray no rain will fall
    On your newly polished
    Four wheeled
    God.

    Envoi.
Beauty is in the eye of the beholder.
Get it out with Optrex.

            Easter Monday 1967

To Robert Graves

Were we
    so be–devilled,
    as to lie fragmented
And the pieces *always* at the foot of
    a woman?

Cannot our
    high thoughts escape from
    the clinging female lichen
    growing on our old bones?

Tho' Spring in his head
    great melting ice caps
    of green ladies
    swamp our Summer logic.

                1967

Opus I

This silent call you make,
A silence so raging loud
I fear the world knows its meaning.
If you fill every corner of a room
Where can I look?
If I close my eyes
    the silence becomes louder!
There is no escape from you.
    The only way out
       is in.

              On train to Bournemouth
              Feb. 1967

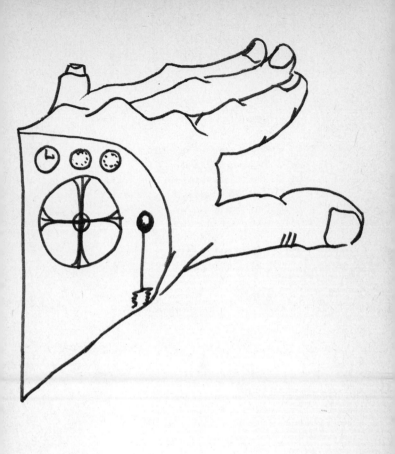

Oberon

The flowers in my garden
    grow down.
Their colour is pain
Their fragrance sorrow.
Into my eyes grow their roots
    feeling for tears
To nourish the black
    hopeless rose
    within me.

Nervous breakdown
Bournemouth
Feb. 1967

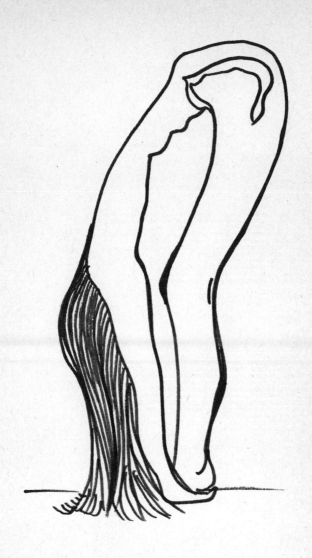

The New Rose

The new rose
    trembles with early beauty
The babe sees the beckoning carmine
    the tiny hand
    clutches the cruel stem.
The babe screams
The rose is silent –
Life is already telling lies.

Orme Court, London
Feb. 1967

Who am I and Why

Values '68

The Prince is dying
'Give him air'.
Headlines! Crisis!
Kennedy Shot!
The assassin captured
Too late! Kennedy dies!
The telegrams flow
And bury the body in – Arlington.
Somewhere in Meekong
A prince of battle
    is blown into bloody meat.
No headlines
No crisis
And only
One telegram.

        Day of Robert Kennedy's
              assassination

Titikaka

Magic green lake
　　　that fell from primeval skies
　　　quenched a burning mountains thirst
　　　and sent a fire king into
　　　　　untimeable slumber.

　　　　　　On a plane over Mexico
　　　　　　　Sept. 1968

Opus II

As I sip
   the midnight dark away
And fading sounds
   from the sleepless radio,
A beating chisel
   cuts your face in my eyes
And Oh!
   how far away is Leicester?
But the stupid wooden cupboard
I can touch from my bed . . . . . .
Have you a wooden cupboard in your room
In Leicester?

           01.00 hrs
              14 Dec. 1968

Love Song

If I could write words
Like leaves on an Autumn Forest floor
What a bonfire my letters would make.
If I could speak words of water
You would drown when I said
'I love you'.

Truth

Seek truth they said
All I find
The seed is lost
The ploughman –
Blind

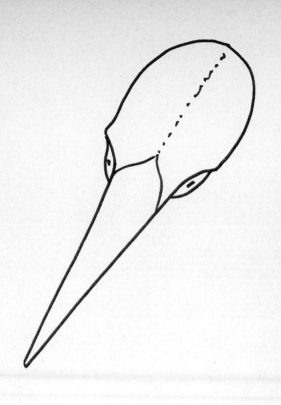

Korea

Why are they lying in some distant land
Why did they go there
Did they *understand* ?
Young men they were
Young men they stay
But why did we send them away, away?

Korea.

Why are they lying in some distant land
Why did they go there
Did they understand?
Young men they were
Young men they stay
Why did we send them away, away?

I once – as a child

I once – as a child – saw Mahatma Ghandi
Walk past the Old Sappers Lines, Climo Road –
He was on his way to Yeroda Gaol. 'He's not
As black as he's painted' said my kind Grandmother –
But I found out he was not painted –
It was his real colour.

Onos

We have cracked the midnight glass
And loosed the racketing star-crazed
      night into the room.
The blind harp sings in late fire-light,
Your hand is decked with white promises.
What wine is this?
There are squirrels chasing in my glass,
Good God! I'm pissed!

D.D.T.

I hear a death rattle
It's in the wine
Each fatal glass
             alas
Is yours . . . . or mine.

Envoi

I hear the vineyards sobbing
Vintage tears
For life, in arrears.

2B or not 2B

When I was small and five
I found a pencil sharpener alive!
He lay in lonely grasses
Looking for work.
I bought a pencil for him
He ate and ate until all that was
Left was a pile of wood dust.
It was the happiest pencil sharpener
I ever had.

2 B or not 2 B

When I was small and five
   I found a pencil sharpner alive!
He lay in lonley grasses
   looking for work.
I bought a pencil for him.
   He ate and ate until all that was
   left was a pile of wood dust.
It was the happiest pencil sharpner
   I ever had.

The Dog Lovers

So they bought you
And kept you in a
Very good home
Central heating
TV
A deep freeze
A *very* good home –
No one to take you
For that lovely long run –
But otherwise
'A *very* good home'.
They fed you Pal and Chum
But not that lovely long run,
Until, mad with energy and boredom
You escaped – and ran and ran and ran
Under a car.
Today they will cry for you –
Tomorrow they will buy another dog.

1970

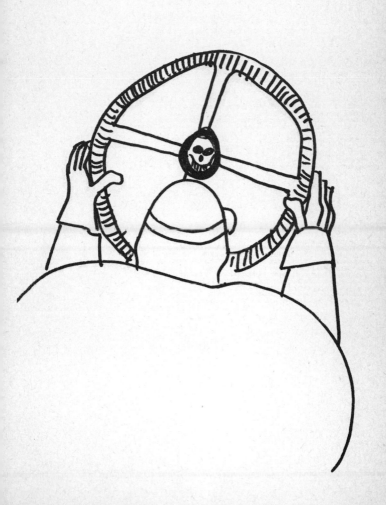

True Love

I saw a purple balloon
  capture a girl one day.
He would not let her go,
  for heaven he strove to take her
  but she was too heavy.
So, he stayed earthbound
  to prove his love, until,
A hundred years later that night
  he died with a bang.
The little girl cried
  for never again
  would she find such a pure love.

May 1970

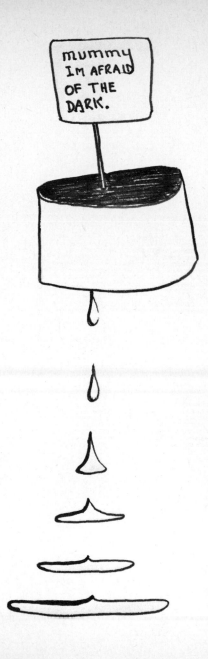

Christmas 1970

A little girl called Silé Javotte
Said 'look at the lovely presents I've got'
While a little girl in Biafra said
'Oh what a lovely slice of bread'.

Christmas 1970

A little girl called Síle Javotte
Said look a the lovely presents I've got
While a little girl in Biafra said
Oh what a lovely slice of bread.

Xmas

Opus III

Your lustrous face
& made me aware
   my incompleteness
In you,
   hidden,
   my sleeping other half.
Help me –
Help me be complete.

                    London
                    Aug '70

England, Home and Beauty for Sale

Beautiful Buildings
No longer stand
In Bloomsbury's
Pleasant Land.
The Land (it's said)
Is sold. Who by?
Oh dearie me
Oh dearie my
A place that teaches
Architectural knowledge
London University College!
So when one stands
And sadly stares
At horrid new buildings
In Bloomsbury's Squares
We know the responsibility's
Theirs.

Envoi

A lot of learning can be a little thing.

Goliath

They chop down 100 ft trees
To make chairs
I bought one
I am six foot one inch.
When I sit in the chair
I'm four foot two.
Did they really chop down a 100 ft tree
To make me look shorter?

Bayswater, London 1971

New Members Welcome

Pull the blinds
 on your emotions
Switch off your face.
Put your love into neutral
This way to the human race.

London, April 1971

Hope

Just when I had made my today
Secure with safe yesterdays
I see tomorrow coming with its pale
    glass star called hope.
It shatters on impact
And falls like splinters of cruel rain
And I see the red oil of life
        running from my wrists
        onto tomorrow's headlines.

        Woy-Woy
        NSW
        Dec. 1971

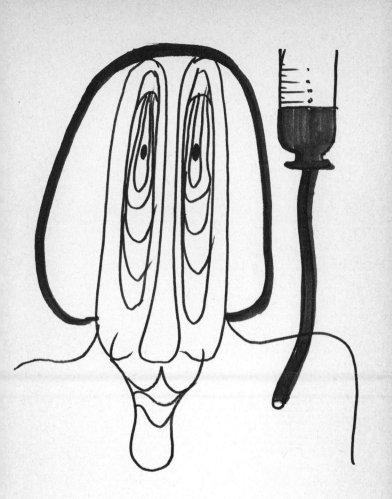

Metropolis

I see barbaric sodium city lamps
  pretending they can see.
They make a new mad darkness.
Beyond their orange pools
  the black endlessness of time beckons,
What, in that unseen dark tomorrow
      is waiting. . . . .
That *iron* tomorrow, coming on
    unknown wheels
Who is the driver,
Will he see me in time?

> Woy-Woy
> NSW
> Oct. 1971

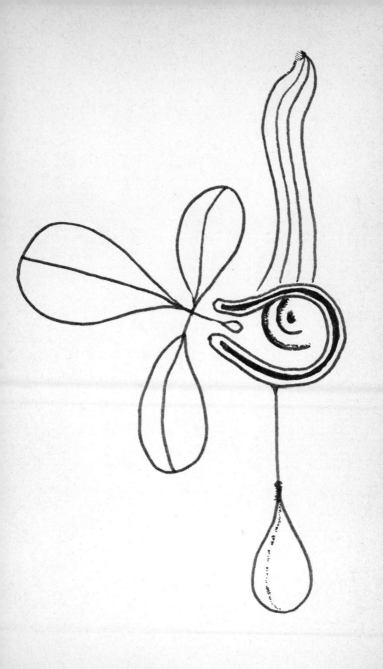

The Future

The young boy stood looking up the road
to the future. In the distance both sides
appeared to converge together. 'That
is due to perspective, when you reach
there the road is as wide as it is here',
said an old wise man. The young
boy set off on the road, but,
as he went on, both sides of the
road converged until he could
go no further. He returned to ask
the old man what to do, but
the old man was dead.

Dublin, Jan. 1972

Unto us . . . . . .

Somewhere at sometime
They committed themselves to me
And so, I was!
Small, but I *was*.
Tiny in shape
Lusting to live
I hung in my pulsing cave.
Soon they knew of me
My mother – my father.
I had no say in my being
I lived on trust
And love
Tho' I couldn't think
Each part of me was saying
A silent 'Wait for me
I will bring you love!'
I was taken
Blind, naked, defenceless
By the hand of one
Whose good name
Was graven on a brass plate
in Wimpole Street,
and dropped on the sterile floor
of a foot operated plastic waste bucket.
There was no Queens Counsel
To take my brief.
The cot I might have warmed
Stood in Harrod's shop window.
When my passing was told
My father smiled.
No grief filled my empty space.

My death was celebrated
With two tickets to see Danny la Rue
Who was pretending to be a woman
Like my mother was.

Tel Aviv, 8th Feb. 1972

Ulster, Derry 1972

When the only colour is black –
    the only sound
    the broken bell
Then talk to me about why.

The Incurable

I have taken maidens
like pots of Vic
and rubbed them into myself
but was never cured
and so, the ailment stays;
I see it carried in each sauntering wench
and forever I seek the cure.
No alchemist has its measure,
no chemist its mix.
Till there comes the medicine
I'll make my own fix.
It may not cure
but will not harm.
It will make magic
but not the balm
and when, in some minded hay loft we lay
I'll not only make a woman –
I will also, make hay.

6 March 1972

Mirror, Mirror

A young Spring-tender girl
   combed her joyous hair
'You are very ugly' said the mirror.
But,
   on her young lips hung
   a smile of dove-secret loveliness,
   for only that morning, had not
   the blind boy said,
'You are beautiful'?

        Somewhere – Sometime
        Somehow.
          April 1972

Plastic Woman

What are you saying
Supermarket shopping lady
In the scarlet telephone box.
Lady with a shopping bag
Full of labelled pollution with secret codes
What are you saying?
Is this your dream booth?
Are you telling some plastic operator
You are Princess Grace
And can he put you through
to Buckingham Palace?
Two decimal pence
Is very little to pay for a dream in Catford.
If only the label on the door didn't say
'Out of Order'.
Shouldn't it be on you?

1972

Spring Song, March 18th 1972

Spring came haunting my garden today –
A song of cold flowers was on the grass.
Tho' I could not see it
I knew the air was coloured
And new songs were
     in the old black bird's throat.
The ground trembled at the thought
     of what was to come!
It was not my garden today,
     it belonged to *itself*.
At the dawn smell of it –
     my children fled the house
And went living in that primitive dimension
     that only they and gardens understand.
My dog too lost his mind
And ran in circle after canine circle
Trying to catch himself –
And do you know what? – He *did*!
It was *that* kind of a day.

        Written in China to
        avoid Income Tax

If I die in War
You remember me
If I live in Peace
You don't.

Irish meeting
slams Heath

Army coup
defeated

SAN SALVADOR, Sunda
sident Fidel Sanchez Hern
''s firmly back in powe
after being held
in an

'Free Angela'
month is May

Morning Star Reporter
to be a month of inten-
igning to free Angela
cal demonstrations
workers

MY FLAT IS IN A POOR

DEATH DEADLINE
EXTENDED
BUENOS A

**GOD MADE NIGHT
BUT
MAN MADE DARKNESS**

MORE ABOUT PENGUINS AND PELICANS

PUCKOON

Spike Milligan

'Spike Milligan's first novel bursts at the seams with superb comic characters involved in unbelievably likely troubles on the Irish border' – *Observer*

'Pops with the erratic brilliance of a careless match in a box of fireworks' – *Daily Mail*

SILLY VERSE FOR KIDS

Spike Milligan

I'm not frightened of Pussy Cats

I'm not frightened of Pussy Cats,
They only eat up mice and rats,
But a Hippopotamus
Could eat the Lotofus!

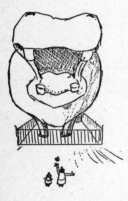

Once again Spike Milligan puts pen to paper and produces a
delightful collection of silly verse – for kids and adults.

A BOOK OF MILLIGANIMALS

Spike Milligan

Do you know what a
Onecan is? Have you
met a Gofongo or the
Bald Twit Lion? Can
you guess what the
Wiggle-Woggle said?

Another collection of
goonish poems and zany
drawings by Spike Milligan.

ADOLF HITLER
My Part in His Downfall
Spike Milligan

'At Victoria Station the R.T.O. gave me a travel warrant, a
white feather and a picture of Hitler marked "This is your
enemy". I searched every compartment, but he wasn't on the
train . . .'

Spike Milligan's on the march, blitzing friend and foe alike with
his uproarious recollections of army life from enlistment to the
landing at Algiers in 1943.
Bathos, pathos, gales of drunken laughter, and insane military
goonery explode in superlative Milliganese.

'It is the most irreverent, hilarious book about the war that I have
ever read' – *Sunday Express*

Not for sale in the U.S.A.